PRINCIPLES OF ARTIFICIAL INTELLIGENCE

DR RENUKA SAGAR

Made with ♥ on the Notion Press Platform
www.notionpress.com

To my family and friends for bringing me joy on the good days and comfort on the bad ones

Contents

Preface

Artificial Intelligence: Foundations of Computational Agents is a book about the science of artificial intelligence (AI). It is structured as a textbook but is designed to be accessible to a wide audience. It combines theory and experiment to develop the science of AI together with its engineering applications. The book follows the dictum of "Everything should be made as simple as possible, but not simpler" and outlines the complexity required to build useful intelligent systems. This edition results from extensive revision throughout the text. AI research is expanding rapidly and the volume of potential new text material is vast. This book is an introductory text on artificial intelligence for advanced undergraduate or graduate students in computer science or related disciplines. It focuses on learning by doing and emphasizes the principles underlying the foundations of computational agents, making them more accessible to students. It includes material on machine learning techniques that have proven successful, but also removes techniques that are less promising. The serious student will gain valuable skills at several levels ranging from expertise in the specification and design of intelligent agents to skills for implementing, testing, and improving real software systems for several challenging application domains.

This edition includes some currently unfashionable material if the problems still remain and the techniques have the potential to form the basis for future research and development. The book can be used as an introductory text on artificial intelligence for advanced undergraduate or graduate students in computer science or related disciplines, appealing to the technically minded. It emphasizes the principles underlying the foundations of computational agents, making them more accessible to students.

The book can be used as an introductory text on artificial intelligence for advanced undergraduate or graduate students in computer science or related disciplines, focusing on learning by doing. It will appeal to the technically minded and provide valuable skills for implementing, testing, and improving real software systems.

Acknowledgements

This book is based on the research in the field of Artificial Intelligence. It is framed as per the curriculum of the undergraduate engineering students. *I am greatful to number of friends, colleagues , and well wishers who encouraged me to start the work, preserve with it, and fnally to publish it.*

The provocation behind writing this book is to provide the basic concepts of Artificial intelligence in an easy,simple and understandable form to the undergraduate students.

I would like to thank my parents and spouses for encouraging and motivating me to write this book.My kids were a source of inspiration and their constant support helped me in completing thisbook.

Above all, I thank GOD, the Almighty, who is the author of knowledge and wisdom for showering unconditional love

CHAPTER ONE

Artificial Intelligence

What is Artificial Intelligence?

A broad field that means different things to different people ? Artificial intelligence (AI) is the study of how to make computers do things which, at the moment, people do better – Rich and Knight, 1991 ? The study of the computations that make it possible to perceive, reason and act – Patrick Henry Winston, 1992 ? AI is a branch of computer science deals with automation of intelligent behavior – Luger & Stubblefield, 1993

? A field of study that seeks to explain and emulate the intelligent behavior in terms of computational processes – Schalkoff, 1990

? The automation of activities that we associate with human thinking – Bellman, 1978 Activities Means: Decision making, problem solving, learning .... ? The study of techniques to make the computers to exhibit some kind of intelligence ? It is the science and engineering of making intelligent machines, especially intelligent computer programs.

It is related to the similar task of using computers to understand human intelligence

i.e., AI deals with the techniques to make computers to exhibit some kind of intelligence.

? **THE AI PROBLEMS**

? Much of the early work in the field focused on formal tasks, such as game playing and theorem proving.

? Samuel wrote a checkers-playing program that not only played games with opponents but also used its experience at those games to improve its later performance. Chess also received a good deal of attention.

? The Logic Theorist was an early attempt to prove mathematical theorems. It was able to prove several theorems. Gelernter's theorem explored another area of mathematics: geometry. Game playing and theorem proving share the property that people who do them well are considered to be displaying intelligence.

? In spite of this, it appeared initially that computers could perform well at those tasks simply by being fast at exploring a large number of solution paths and then selecting the best one. It was thought that this process required very little knowledge and could therefore be programmed easily.

Another early work in AI focused is on the sort of problems solving called commonsense reasoning. It includes reasoning about physical objects and their relationships to each other. To investigate this sort of reasoning, Newell, Shaw, and Simon built the General Problem Solver (GPS) - here only simple tasks were selected.

? AI research progressed and techniques for handling larger amounts of world knowledge were developed. These include perception – vision and speech, natural language understanding, and problems solving in specialized domains such as medical diagnosis and chemical analysis and are referred as Mundane tasks.

? In addition to mundane tasks, people can also perform specialized tasks in which carefully acquired expertise is necessary. Examples of such tasks include engineering design, scientific discovery, medical diagnosis and financial planning. Figure below lists some of the tasks that are targets of work in AI.

? As a result, the problem areas where AI is now flourishing most as a practical discipline are primarily the domains that require only specialized expertise without the assistance of commonsense knowledge.

Some of the Task Domains of AI

? Mundane Tasks

– Perception

• Vision

• Speech

– Natural Languages

• Understanding

• Generation

• Translation

– Common sense reasoning

– Robot Control

? Formal Tasks

– Games Playing

• Chess

• Backgammon

• Checkers - Go
– Mathematics
• Geometry
• Logic
• Integral calculus
Theorem Proving
• General Problem Solving
? Expert Tasks (require specialized skills and training)
– Engineering
• Design
• Fault finding
• Manufacturing planning
– Scientific Analysis
– Medical Diagnosis
– Financial Analysis
Note: AI is concerned with automating both Mundane and Expert tasks

? **THE UNDERLYING ASSUMPTION**

The heart of research in artificial intelligence lies what Newell and Simon [1976] call the physical symbol system hypothesis. They define a Physical symbol system as follows:

? A physical symbol system consist of a set of entities called symbols, which are physical patterns that can occur as components of another type of entity called an expression or symbol structure. Thus, a symbol structure is composed of a number of instances or tokens of symbols related in some physical way. At any instant of time the system will contain a collection of these symbol structures.

? In addition to these structures, the system also contains a collection of processes that operate on expressions to produce other expressions: processes of creation, modification, reproduction and destruction. A physical symbol system is a machine that produces through time, an evolving collection of symbol structures.

? The physical Symbol System Hypothesis can be stated as – A physical symbol system has the necessary and sufficient means for general intelligent action.

? The truth of this hypothesis can be determined only by experimentation. Computers provide the perfect medium for this experimentation since they can be programmed to simulate any physical symbol system. This ability of computers to serve as arbitrary symbol manipulators was noticed very early in the history of computing by Lady Lovelace about Babbage's proposed Analytical Engine in 1842.

? The operating mechanism can even be thrown into action independently of any object to operate upon. As it has become increasingly easy to build computing machines, so it has become increasingly possible to conduct empirical investigations of the physical symbol system hypothesis. In each such investigation, a particular task that might be regarded as requiring intelligence is selected. A program to perform the task is proposed and then tested. We have not been completely successful at creating programs that perform all the selected tasks.

Evidence in support of the physical symbol system hypothesis has come not only from areas such as game playing, but also from areas such as visual perception, where it is more tempting to suspect the influence of sub-symbolic processes. However, sub-symbolic models such as neural networks are beginning to challenge symbolic ones at such low-level tasks.

? **WHAT IS AN AI TECHNIQUE?**

Artificial intelligence problems span a very broad spectrum. There are techniques that are appropriate for the solution of a variety of these problems.

One of the few hard and fast results to come out of the first three decades of AI research is that

intelligence requires knowledge. The knowledge possesses some properties as follows:

? It is voluminous

? It is hard to characterize accurately

? It is constantly changing

? It differs from data being organized in a way that corresponds to the ways it will be used

Here, it is concluded that an AI technique is a method that exploits knowledge that should be

represented in such a way that:

? The knowledge captures generalizations means that, it is not necessary to represent separately each individual situation. Instead, situations that share important properties are grouped together. If knowledge does not have this property, excessive amounts of memory and updating will be require, then called as data rather than knowledge.

? It can be understood by people who must provide it. Although for many programs, the bulk of the data can be acquired automatically, for example by taking readings from a variety of instruments.

? It can easily be modified to correct errors and to reflect changes in the world and in our world view.

? It can be used in many situations even if it is not totally accurate or complete.

? It can be used to help overcome its own complete volume by helping to narrow the range of possibilities.

Although AI techniques must be designed in keeping with these constraints imposed by Al problems, there is some degree of independence between problems and problem-solving techniques. It is possible to solve Al problems without using AI techniques and it is possible to apply AI techniques to the solution of non-Al problems.

In order to characterize AI techniques as problem-independent way as possible, let us consider some problems.

? Tic-Tac-Toe problem

Here, presented a series of three programs to play tic-tac-toe. The programs in this series increase in:

The clarity of their knowledge

? Their complexity

? Their use of generalizations

? The extensibility of their approach. Thus, they move toward being representations of what we call AI techniques.

Program 1

Data Structures:

Board A nine-element vector representing the board, where the elements of the vector correspond to the board positions as follows:

1	2	3
4	5	6
7	8	9

An element contains the value 0 if the corresponding square is blank. 1 if it is filled with an X, or 2 if it is filled with an O.

Movetable A large vector of 19,683 elements (39), each element of which is a nine-element vector.

The contents of this-vector are chosen specifically to allow the algorithm to work.

Algorithm:

To make a move, do the following:

1. View the vector Board as a ternary (base three) number. Convert it to a decimal number.
2. Use the number computed in step 1 as an index into Movetable and access the vector stored there.
3. The vector selected in step 2 represents the way the board will look after the move that should be made. So set Board equal to that vector.

Comments:

This program is very efficient in terms of time. And, in theory, it could play an optimal game of tic-tac- toe. But it has several disadvantages:

? It takes a lot of space to store the table of each move

? Have to do a lot of work specifying all the entries in the movetable.

? It is very unlikely that all the required movetable entries can be determined and entered without any errors.

If we want to extend the game, say to three dimensions, we would have to start from scratch, since 327 board positions would have to be stored, occupies large memory.

Program 2

Data Structures:

Board A nine-element vector representing the board, as described for Program 1. But instead of using the numbers 0, 1 or 2 in each element, we store 2 is blank, 3 for X and 5 for O.

Turn An integer indicating which move of the game is about to be played; 1 indicates the first move, 9 the last.

Algorithm:

The main algorithm uses three sub-procedures:

Make 2 Returns 5 if the center square of the board is blank, that is, if Board [5] = 2. Otherwise, this function returns any blank Noncorner Square – 2, 4, 6, or 8.

Posswin (p) Returns 0 if player p cannot win on his next move; otherwise, it returns the number of the square that constitutes a winning move. This function will enable the program both to win and to block the opponent's win. Posswin operates by checking, one at a time, each of the rows, columns, and diagonals. Because of the way values are numbered it can test an entire row/column/diagonal to see if it is a possible win by multiplying the values of its squares together. If the product is 18 (3 x 3 x 2), then X can win (means one of the squares is empty). If the product is 50 (5 x 5 x 2), then O can win (means one of the squares is empty). If we find a winning row, we determine which element is blank, and return the number of that square.

Go (n) Makes a move in square n. This procedure sets Board[n] to 3 if Turn is odd, or 5 if Turn is even. It also increments Turn by one.

The algorithm has a built-in strategy for each move. It makes the odd-numbered moves if it is playing X, the even-numbered moves if it is playing O. The strategy for each turn is as follows:

Turn= 1 Go(1) (upper left corner).

Turn= 2 If Board [5] is blank, Go(5), else Go(1).

Turn= 3 If Board [9] is blank, Go(9), else Go(3).

Turn= 4 If Posswin(X) is not 0, then Go(Posswin(X)) [i.e., block opponent's win], else Go(Make2).

Turn= 5 If Posswin(X) is not 0 then Go(Posswin(X))[i.e., win] else if Posswin(O) is not 0, then Go(Posswin(O)) [i.e., block win], else if Board[7] is blank, then Go(7), else Go(3). [Here the program is trying to make a fork.]

Turn= 6 If Posswin(O) is not 0 then Go (Posswin(O)), else if Posswin(X) is not 0, then Go(Posswin(X)), else Go(Make2).

Turn= 7 If Posswin(X) is not 0 then Go(Posswin(X)). else if Posswin(O) is not 0, then Go(Posswin(O)). Else go anywhere that is blank.

Turn= 8 If Posswin(O) is not 0 then Go(Posswin(O)), else if Posswin(X) is not 0, then Go(Posswin(X)), else go anywhere that is blank.

Turn= 9 Same as Turn=7.

Program 2 – A

This program is identical to program 2 except for the one change in the representation of the board and is as follows:

8	3	4
1	5	9
6	7	2

Here, numbering of the board produces a magic square: all the rows, columns, and diagonals sum up to
15. This means that we can simplify the process of checking for a possible win. In addition to marking the board as moves are made, we keep a list, for each player, of the squares in which he or she has played. To check for a possible win for one player, we consider each pair of squares owned by that player and compute the difference between 15 and the sum of the two squares. If this difference is not positive or if it is greater than 9, then the original two squares were not collinear and so can be ignored. Otherwise, if the square representing the difference is blank (1 to 9 squares), a move there will produce a win. This shows how the choice of representation can have a major impact on the efficiency of a problem-solving program.

- **Program 3**

Data Structures

BoardPosition: A structure containing a nine-element vector representing the board, a list of board positions that could result from the next move, and a number representing an estimate of how likely the board position is to lead to an ultimate win for the player to move.

Algorithm:

To decide on the next move, look ahead at the board positions that result from each possible move. Decide which position is best (as described below), make the move that leads to that position, and assign the rating of that best move to the current position.

To decide which of a set of board positions is best, do the following for each of them:

1. See if it is a win. If so, call it the best by giving it the highest possible rating.

2. Otherwise, consider all the moves the opponent could make next. See which of them is worst for us (by recursively calling this procedure). Assume the opponent will make that move. Whatever rating that moves has, assign it to the node we are considering.

3. The best node is then the one with the highest rating.

This algorithm will look ahead at various sequences of moves in order to find a sequence that leads to a win. It attempts to maximize the likelihood of winning, while assuming that the opponent will try to minimize that likelihood. This algorithm is called the minimax procedure.

? Question Answering problem

Here, programs that read in English text and then answer questions also stated in English, about that text. This is more difficult to state formally and precisely what our problem is and what constitutes correct solutions to it. For example, suppose that the input text were just the single sentence

Example 1:

Russia massed troops on the Czech border.

Then either of the following question-answering dialogues might occur with the POLITICS program:

Dialogue 1

Q: Why did Russia do this?

A: Because Russia thought that it could take political control of Czechoslovakia by sending troops. Q: What should the United States do?

A: The United States should intervene (interfere) militarily.

Dialogue 2

Q: Why did Russia do this?

A: Because Russia wanted to increase its political influence over Czechoslovakia. Q: What should the United States do?

A: The United States should denounce (condemn) the Russian action in the United Nations.

? In the POLITICS program, answers were constructed by considering both the input text and a separate model of the beliefs and actions of various political entities, including Russia. When the model is changed, the system's answers alsochange.

The general point here is that defining what it means to produce a correct answer to a question may be very hard.

Example 2:

Mary went shopping for a new coat. She found a red one she really liked. When she got it home, she discovered that it went perfectly with her favorite dress.

Attempt to answer each of the following questions with each program:

Q1: What did Mary go shopping for? Q2: What did Mary find that she liked? Q3: Did Mary buy anything?

Program 1

This program is to attempt to answer questions using the literal text. It simply matches text fragments in the questions against the input text.

Data structures

Question patterns: A set of templates that match common question forms and produce patterns to be used to match against inputs. Templates and patterns are paired so that if a template matches successfully against an input question then its associated text patterns are used to try finding appropriate answers in the text. For example, if the template "who did x y" matches an input question, then the text patterns "x, y, z" is matched against the text and the value of z is given as the answer to the question.

Text The input text stored simply as a long character string.

Question The current question also stored as a character string.

Algorithm

To answer a question, do the following:

1. Compare each element of Question Patterns, the question and all those that match successfully to generate a set of text patterns.
2. Pass each of these patterns through a substitution process that generates alternative forms of verbs so that, for example, "go" in a question might match "went" in the text. This step generates a new, expanded set of text patterns.
3. Apply each of these text patterns to text, and collect all the resulting answers.
4. Reply with the set of answers just collected.

Answers:

Q1: The template "what did x y" matches this question and generates the text pattern "Mary go shopping for z." After the pattern-substitution step, this pattern is expanded to a set of patterns including "Mary goes shopping for z," and "Mary went shopping for z." the latter pattern matches the input text; the program, using a convention that variables match the longest possible string up to a sentence delimiter (such as a period), assigns z the value, "a new coat," which is given as the answer.

Q2: Unless the template set is very large, allowing for the insertion of the object of "find" between it and the modifying phrase "that she liked," the insertion of the word "really" in the text, and the substitution of "she" for "Mary," this question is hot answerable. If all of these variations are accounted for and the question can be answered, then the response is "a red one".

Q3: Since no answer to this question is contained in the text, no answer will be found.

Program 2

This program first converts the input text into a structured internal from that attempt to capture the meaning of the sentences. It also converts questions into that form. It finds answers by matching structured forms against each other.

Data structures

EnglishKnow: A description of the words, grammar, and appropriate semantic interpretations of a large enough subset of English to account for the input texts that the system will see. This knowledge of English is used both to map input sentences into an internal, meaning-oriented form and to map from such internal forms back into English. The former process is used when English text is being read; the latter is used to generate English answers from the meaning-oriented from that constitutes the program's knowledge base.

Inputtext The input text in character form.

StructuredText A Structured representation of the content of the input text. This Structure attempts to capture the essential Knowledge contained in the text, independently of the exact way that the Knowledge was stated in English

A Structured Representation of a sentence:

Event 2

Instance: Finding

Tense: Past

Agent: Mary

Object: Thing 1

Thing 1

Instance: Coat
Color: Red

Event 2
Instance: Liking
Tense: Past
Modifier: Much
Object: Thing 1
InputQuestion The input question in character form.
StructQuestions A structured representation of the content of the user's question. The structure is the same as the one used to represent the content of the input text.

Algorithm:

Convert the input text into structured form using the Knowledge contained in English Know. This may require considering several different potential structures, for a variety of reasons, including the fact that English words can be ambiguous, English grammatical structures can be ambiguous, and pronouns may have several possible antecedents. Then, to answer a question, do the following:

1. Convert the question to structured form, again using the Knowledge contained in English Know. Use some special marker in the structure to indicate the part of the structure that should be returned as the answer. This marker will often correspond to the occurrence of a question word (like "who" or "what") in the sentence. The exact way in which this marking gets done depends on the form chosen for representing structured Text.
2. Match this structured form against Structured Text.
3. Return as the answer those parts of the text that match the requested segment of the question.

Answers:

Q1: This question is answered straightforwardly with, "a new coat" Q2: This one also is answered successfully with, "a red coat".

Q3: This one, though, cannot be answered, since there is no direct response to it in the text.

Program 3

This program converts the input text into a structured form that contains the meanings of the sentences in the text, and then it combines that form with other structured forms that describe prior knowledge about the objects and situations involved in the text. It answers questions using this augmented knowledge structure.

Data structures

World Model: A Structured representation of background world Knowledge. This structure contains Knowledge about objects, actions and situations that are described in the input text. This Structure is used to construct Integrated Text from the input text. For example, Figure below shows an example of a Structure that represents the systems Knowledge about shopping. In the case of this text, for example, M is a coat and M' is a red coat. Branches in the figure describe alternative paths through the script.

The Algorithm:

Convert the input Text into structured form using both the Knowledge contained in English Know and that contained in world model. The number possible structures will usually be greater now than it was in program 2 because so much more Knowledge is being used. Sometimes, though, it may be possible to consider fewer possibilities by using the additional knowledge to filter the alternatives.

Shopping script:

Roles: C (customer), S (salesperson) Props: M (merchandise), D (dollars)

Location: L (a store)

To answer a question, do the following:

1. Convert the question to structured form as in program 2 but use WorldModel necessary to resolve any ambiguities that may arise.
2. Match this structured form against Integrated Text.
3. Return as the answer those parts of the text that match the requested segment of the question.

A Shopping Script diagram

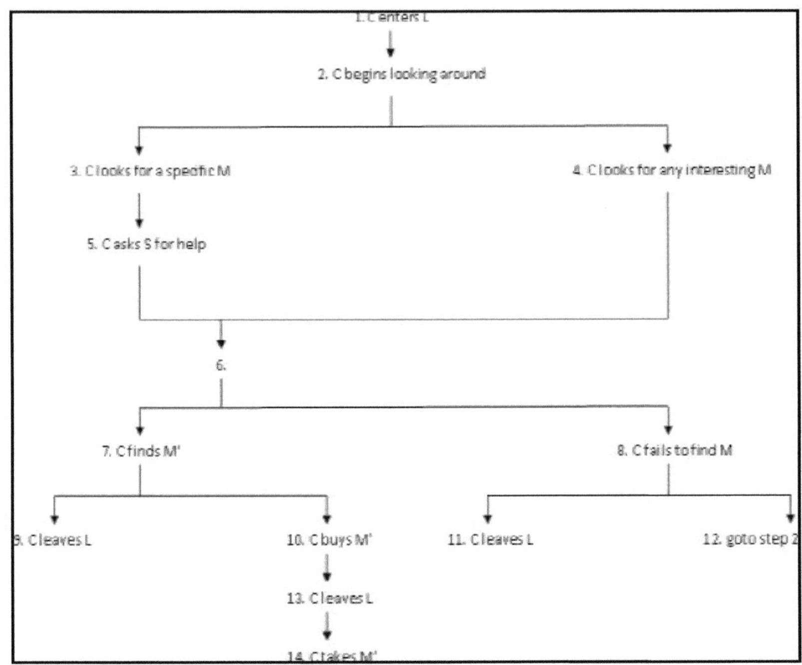

Answers:

Q1: Same as Program 2.

Q2: Same as Program 2.

Q3: Now this question can be answered. The shopping script is instantiated for this text, and because of the last sentence, the path through step 14 of the script is the one that is used in forming the representation of the text. When the script is instantiated M1 is bound to the structure representing the red coat. After the script has been instantiated, Integrated Text contains several events. That are taken from the script but that are not described in the original text, including the event "Mary buys a red coat" (from step 10 of the script). Thus, using the integrated text as the basis for question answering allows the program to respond "she bought a red coat".

We can conclude that these problems illustrate important AI techniques:

? Search- Provides a way of solving problems for which no more direct approach is available.

? Use of Knowledge- Provides a way of solving complex problems by exploiting the structures of the objects that are involved.

? Abstractions – Provides a way of separating important features and variations from the many unimportant ones.

? THE LEVELS OF THE MODEL / (STATE OF THE ART)

We must ask ourselves, what is our goal in trying to produce programs that do the intelligent things that people do? Or, are we trying to produce programs that do the tasks the same way people do? Or, are we attempting to produce programs that simply do the tasks in whatever way appear easiest? There have been AI projects motivated by each of these goals.

These programs are divided into two classes –

? Programs in the first class attempt to solve problems that do not really fit definition of an AI task. They are problems that a computer cloud easily solves.

? Example is Elementary Perceiver and Memorizer (EPAM) [Feigenbaum, 1963], which memorized associated pairs of nonsense syllables. Memorizing pairs of nonsense syllables is easy for a computer. But this task is hard for people.

? The programs in the second class attempt to model human performance and are within AI definitions. Reasons for this are:

? **To test psychological theories of human performance:** An example of a program that was written for this reason is PARRY [Colby, 1975], which exploited a model of human paranoid behavior to simulate the conversational behavior of a paranoid (Suspicious) person. Themodel was good enough that when several psychologists were given the opportunity to converse with the program via a terminal, they diagnosed its behavior as paranoid.

? **To enable computers to understand human reasoning:** For example, for a computer to be able to read a newspaper story and then answer a question, such as "why did the terrorists kill the hostages?" Its program must be able to simulate the reasoning processes of people.

To enable people to understand computer reasoning: In many circumstances, people are reluctant to rely on the output of a computer unless they can understand how the machine arrived at its result. If the computer's reasoning process is similar to that of people, then producing an acceptable explanation is much easier.

? **To exploit what knowledge we can glean (Gather) from people:** Since people are the best- known performers of most of the tasks with which we are dealing, it makes a lot of sense to look to them for clues as to how to produce.

? The following are the disciplines that contributed ideas, new points, and techniques to AI:

? **Philosophy: (**428BC- Present)
1. Can formal rules be used to draw valid conclusions?
2. How does the mental mind arise from a physical brain?
3. Where does knowledge come from?
4. How does knowledge lead to action?

? **Mathematics**
1. What are the formal rules to draw valid conclusions?
2. What can be computed?
3. How do we reason with uncertain information?

? **Economics**
1. How should we make decisions so as to maximize pay off?
2. How should we do this when others may not go along?
3. How should we do this when the pay off may be far in the feature?

? **Neuroscience**
How do brains process information?

? Psychology
How do humans and animals think & act?

? **Computer Engineer**
How can we an efficient as computer?

? Computer Theory and Cybernetics
How can computer operate under their own control?

? **Linguistic**
How does language relate to thought?
Note: The questions under each of the above foundations, shows that, what exactly their contributions

? **The History / Early works of AI:**

? The first work in AI was done by McCalloch and Pitts (1943), who proposed artificial neurons. They worked on three sources:
1. Knowledge of the basic Physiology.
2. Functions of neurons in the brain

A formal analysis of propositional logic and turing's theory of computations.

? Later in 1949, Donald Hebb demonstrated a simple updating rule for modifying the connection strengths between neurons, called Hebbbian Learning.

? Alan Turing (1950), was the first to articulate the complete vision of AI in his article (1950) – "Computing Machinery and Intelligence", he introduced the Turing Test, Machine learning, genetic algorithms and reinforcement learning.

? John McCarthy of Dart Month College called the father of AI, introduced automata theory, neural networks, and the study of intelligence (1956). Also he designed the language LISP in 1958.

? Newell and Simon (1976) designed a program called General Problem Solver (GPS) that imitated human problem solving protocols. GPS was the first program to embody the "Thinking humanly" approach.

? Rosenblatt (1962) developed perceptrons by enhancing the Hebban learning algorithm.

? DENDRAL and MYCIN were the two expert systems – one for Molecule structure analysis and the other for diagnose the blood infections, developed during 1969, at MIT.

? Recent years have seen a revolution in both the content and the methodology of work in AI.

? Complete Agent architecture proposed during 1990 aims to understand the workings of agents embedded real environments, with continuous sensory inputs. One of the most important environments for intelligent agents in the Internet.

? AI Systems have become so common in web-based applications including search engines, recommended systems, and website construction systems.

? **What can AI do today?**

These are just examples of AI systems that exist today.

? **Autonomous Planning and scheduling:** NASA'S Remote Agent program became the first on board autonomous planning program to control the scheduling of operations for a spacecraft (Jonsson et.al., 2000), such as detection, diagnosis and recovery from problems as that occurred.

? **Game Planning:** IBM'S Deep Blue, Became the first computer to defect the world champion in chess match when it beated Garry Karpasov (1997), the value of IBM'S stock increased by $18 billion.

? **Autonomous Control:** The ALVINN computer vision system was trained to steer a car to keep it following a lane (driving autonomously 98% of the time from Pittsburgh to San Diego, 2850 miles)

? **Diagnosis:** Medical diagnosis programs based on probabilistic analysis have been able to perform at the level of an expert physician is several areas of medicine.

? **Logistics Planning:** During the Persian Gulf crisis of 1991, US forces deployed a Dynamic Analysis and Re-planning Tool, (DART) in1994, to do automated logistics planning and scheduling for transportation. This involved up to 50,000 vehicles, cargo, and people at a time, and had to account for starting points, destinations, routes andconflict resolution among all parameters.Robotics: Many surgeries now use robot assistants in microsurgery. Ex: HIPNAV (1996) is a system that uses computer vision techniques to create a three- dimensional model of a patient's internal anatomy and the uses robotic control to guide the insertion of a hip replacement prosthesis.

? **Language Understanding and Problem Solving:** PROVERB (1999) is a program that solves crossword puzzles setter than most humans.

? CRITERIA FOR SUCCESS

? One of the most important questions to answer in any scientific or engineering research project is "How will we know if we have succeeded?" Artificial intelligence is no exception. How will we know if we have constructed a machine that is intelligent? Can we do anything to measure our progress? Yes ? In 1950, Alan Turing proposed the following method for determining whether a machine can think. His method has since become known as the Turing Test. To conduct this test, we need two people and the machine to be evaluated. One person plays the role of the interrogator, who is in a separate room from the computer and the other person. The interrogator can ask questions of either the person or the computer by typing questions and receiving typed responses. However, the interrogator knows them only as A and B and aims to determine which the person is and which the machine is. The goal of the machines is to fool the interrogator into believing that it is the person. If the machine succeeds at this, then we will conclude that the machine can think. The machine is allowed to do whatever it can to fool the interrogator. So, for example, if asked the questions "How much is 12,324 times 73,981?" it could wait several minutes and then respond with the wrong answer [Turing, 1963].

? We are forced to conclude that the question of whether a machine has intelligence or can think is too vague to answer precisely. But it is often possible to construct a computer program that meets some performance standard for a particular task. That does not mean that the program does the task in the best possible way. It means only that we understand at least one way of doing at least part of a task.

? SOME GENERAL REFERENCES

There is a great many sources of information about artificial intelligence.

? First, will have some survey books: The broadest are the multi-volume handbook of artificial intelligence [Barr et al.. 1981] and Encyclopedia of artificial intelligence [Shapiro and Eckroth, 1987], both of which contain articles on each of the major topics in the field.

? Four other books that provide good overviews of the field are artificial intelligence [Winston, 1984], introduction to artificial intelligence [Charniak and McDermott, 1985], Logical Foundations of artificial intelligence [Genesereth and Nilsson, 1987], and The Elements of artificial intelligence [Tanimoto, 1987] of more restricted scope is principles of artificial intelligence [Nilsson, 1980], which contains a formal treatment of some general- purpose AI techniques.

? Most the work conducted in AI has been originally reported in journal articles, conference proceedings or technical reports. But some of the most interesting of these papers have later appeared in special collections published as books. Computer and Thought [Feigenbaum and Feldman, 1963] is a very early collection of this sort. Later ones include Simon and Siklossy[1972], Schank and Colby [1973], Bobrow and Collins [1975], waterman and Hayes- Roth[1978], Findler [1979],Webber and Nilsson [1981], Halpern[1986], Shrobe [1988], and several others that are mentioned in later chapter in connection with specific topics. For newer AI paradigms the book fundamentals of the new artificial intelligence [Toshinori Munakata, 1998] is a good one.

? The major journal of AI research is called simply Artificial Intelligence. In addition, Cognitive science is devoted to papers dealing with the overlapping areas of psychology, linguistics, and artificial intelligence. AI magazine is a more ephemeral, less technical magazine that is published by the American Association for artificial intelligence (AAAI). IEEE Expert, IEEE Transactions on Systems, Man and Cybernetics, IEEE Transactions on Neural Networks and several other journals publish papers on a board spectrum of AI application domains.

? Since 1969, there has been a major AI conference, the International Joint Conference on Artificial Intelligence (IJCAI), held every two years. The proceedings of these conferences give a good picture of the work that was taking place at the time. The other important AI conference, held three out of every four years starting in 1980, is sponsored by the AAAI, and its proceedings, too, are published.

? In addition of these general references, there exists a whole array of papers and books describing individual AI projects.

? ONE FINAL WORD AND BEYOND

Solving the problems is the topic of discussion in AI. We need methods to help us solve AI's serious

dilemma:

? An AI system must contain a lot of knowledge if it is to handle anything

? But as the amount of knowledge grows, it becomes harder to access the appropriate things when needed, so more knowledge must be added to help. But now there is even more knowledge to manage, so more must be added, and so forth.

? AI is still young discipline possibly in the sense that little has been achieved as compared to what was expected.

? Robots form the ultimate test-bed for AI. Finally one should not forget that research in AI is multidisciplinary.

CHAPTER TWO

Rules for Knowledge Representation

- One way to represent knowledge is by using rules that express what must happen or what does happen when certain conditions are met.
- Rules are usually expressed in the form of IF . . . THEN . . . statements, such as: IF A THEN B This can be considered to have a similar logical meaning as the following: A→B
- A is called the antecedent and B is the consequent in this statement.
- In expressing rules, the consequent usually takes the form of an action or a conclusion.
- In other words, the purpose of a rule is usually to tell a system (such as an expert system) what to do in certain circumstances, or what conclusions to draw from a set of inputs about the current situation.
- In general, a rule can have more than one antecedent, usually combined either by AND or by OR (logically the same as the operators ∧and ∨).
- Similarly, a rule may have more than one consequent, which usually suggests that there are multiple actions to be taken.
- In general, the antecedent of a rule compares an object with a possible value, using an operator.
- For example, suitable antecedents in a rule might be IF x > 3

  IF name is "Bob" IF weather is cold

- Here, the objects being considered are x, name, and weather; the operators are ">" and "is", and the values are 3, "Bob," and cold.
- Note that an object is not necessarily an object in the real-world sense—the weather is not a real world object, but rather a state or condition of the world.

- An object in this sense is simply a variable that represents some physical object or state in the real world.
- An example of a rule might be

  IF name is "Bob" AND weather is cold
  THEN tell Bob 'Wear a coat'

- This is an example of a recommendation rule, which takes a set of inputsand gives advice as a result.
- The conclusion of the rule is actually an action, and the action takes the form of a recommendation to Bob that he should wear a coat.
- In some cases, the rules provide more definite actions such as "move left" or "close door," in which case the rules are being used to represent directives.
- Rules can also be used to represent relations such as: IF temperature is below 0

  THEN weather is cold

Rule-Based Systems

- **Rule-based systems** or **production systems** are computer systems that use rules to provide recommendations or diagnoses, or to determine a course of action in a particular situation or to solve a particular problem.
- A rule-based system consists of a number of components:
  - a database of rules (also called a **knowledge base**)
  - a database of facts
  - an **interpreter**, or **inference engine**
- In a rule-based system, the knowledge base consists of a set of rules that represent the knowledge that the system has.
- The database of facts represents inputs to the system that are used to derive conclusions, or to cause actions.
- The interpreter, or inference engine, is the part of the system that controls the process of deriving conclusions. It uses the rules and facts,

and combines them together to draw conclusions.

- Using deduction to reach a conclusion from a set of antecedents is called **forward chaining**.
- An alternative method, **backward chaining**, starts from a conclusion and tries to show it by following a logical path backward from the conclusion to a set of antecedents that are in the database of facts.
- Forward Chaining

  - Forward chaining employs the system starts from a set of facts, and a set of rules, and tries to find a way of using those rules and facts to deduce a conclusion or come up with a suitable course of action.
  - This is known as **data-driven reasoning** because the reasoning starts from a set of data and ends up at the goal, which is the conclusion.
  - When applying forward chaining, the first step is to take the facts in the fact database and see if any combination of these matches all the antecedents of one of the rules in the rule database.
  - When all the antecedents of a rule are matched by facts in the database, then this rule is **triggered**.
  - Usually, when a rule is triggered, it is then **fired**, which means its conclusion is added to the facts database. If the conclusion of the rule that has fired is an action or a recommendation, then the system may cause that action to take place or the recommendation to be made.
  - For example, consider the following set of rules that is used to control an elevator in a three-story building:

Rule 1

IF on first floor and button is pressed on first floor
THEN open door

Rule 2

IF on first floor
AND button is pressed on second floor THEN go to second floor

Rule 3

IF on first floor
AND button is pressed on third floor THEN go to third floor

Rule 4

IF on second floor
AND button is pressed on first floor
AND already going to third floor
THEN remember to go to first floor later

- This represents just a subset of the rules that would be needed, but we can use it to illustrate how forward chaining works.
- Let us imagine that we start with the following facts in our database:

Fact 1

At first floor

Fact 2

Button pressed on third floor

Fact 3

Today is Tuesday

- Now the system examines the rules and finds that Facts 1 and 2 match the antecedents of Rule 3. Hence, Rule 3 fires, and its conclusion "Go to third floor" is added to the database of facts. Presumably, this results in the elevator heading toward the third floor.
- Note that Fact 3 was ignored altogether because it did not match the antecedents of any of the rules.
- Now let us imagine that the elevator is on its way to the third floor and has reached the second floor, when the button is pressed on the first floor. The fact Button pressed on first floor
- Is now added to the database, which results in Rule 4 firing.

- Now let us imagine that later in the day the facts database contains the following information:

Fact 1

At first floor

Fact 2

Button pressed on second floor

Fact 3

Button pressed on third floor

- In this case, two rules are triggered—Rules 2 and 3. In such cases where there is more than one possible conclusion, **conflict resolution** needs to be applied to decide which rule to fire.

• Conflict Resolution

- In a situation where more than one conclusion can be deduced from a set of facts, there are a number of possible ways to decide which rule to fire.
- For example, consider the following set of rules: IF it is cold

THEN wear a coat IF it is cold
THEN stay at home IF it is cold
THEN turn on the heat

- If there is a single fact in the fact database, which is "it is cold," then clearly there are three conclusions that can be derived. In some cases, it might be fine to follow all three conclusions, but in many cases the conclusions are incompatible.
- In one conflict resolution method, rules are given priority levels, and when a conflict occurs, the rule that has the highest priority is fired, as in the following example:

IF patient has pain
THEN prescribe painkillers priority 10 IF patient has chest pain
THEN treat for heart disease priority 100

- Here, it is clear that treating possible heart problems is more important than just curing the pain.
- An alternative method is the **longest-matching strategy**. This method involves firing the conclusion that was derived from the longest rule.
- For example:

IF patient has pain
THEN prescribe painkiller IF patient has chest pain AND patient is over 60
AND patient has history of heart conditions THEN take to emergency room

- Here, if all the antecedents of the second rule match, then this rule's conclusion should be fired rather than the conclusion of the first rule because it is a more specific match.
- A further method for conflict resolution is to fire the rule that has matched the facts most recently added to the database.
- In each case, it may be that the system fires one rule and then stops, but in many cases, the system simply needs to choose a suitable ordering for the rules because each rule that matches the facts needs to be fired at some point.

- Meta Rules
    - In designing an expert system, it is necessary to select the conflict resolution method that will be used, and quite possibly it will be necessary to use different methods to resolve different types of conflicts.
    - For example, in some situations it may make most sense to use the method that involves firing the most recently added rules.
    - This method makes most sense in situations in which the timeliness of data is important. It might be, for example, that as research in a particular field of medicine develops, and new rules are added to the

system that contradicts some of the older rules.

- It might make most sense for the system to assume that these newer rules are more accurate than the older rules.
- It might also be the case, however, that the new rules have been added by an expert whose opinion is less trusted than that of the expert who added the earlier rules.
- In this case, it clearly makes more sense to allow the earlier rules priority.
- This kind of knowledge is called **meta knowledge**—knowledge about knowledge. The rules that define how conflict resolution will be used, and how other aspects of the system itself will run, are called **meta rules.**
- The knowledge engineer who builds the expert system is responsible for building appropriate meta knowledge into the system (such as "expert A is to be trusted more than expert B" or "any rule that involves drug X is not to be trusted as much as rules that do not involve X").
- Meta rules are treated by the expert system as if they were ordinary rules but are given greater priority than the normal rules that make up the expert system.

In this way, the meta rules are able to override the normal rules, if necessary, and are certainly able to control the conflict resolution process.

- Backward Chaining

  - Forward chaining applies a set of rules and facts to deduce whatever conclusions can be derived, which is useful when a set of facts are present, but you do not know what conclusions you are trying to prove.
  - Forward chaining can be inefficient because it may end up proving a number of conclusions that are not currently interesting.
  - In such cases, where a single specific conclusion is to be proved, **backward chaining** is more appropriate.
  - In backward chaining, we start from a conclusion, which is the **hypothesis** we wish to prove, and we aim to show how that conclusion can be reached from the rules and facts in the database.

- The conclusion we are aiming to prove is called a **goal**, and so reasoning in this way is known as **goal-driven reasoning**.
- Backward chaining is often used in formulating plans.
- A plan is a sequence of actions that a program decides to take to solve a particular problem.
- Backward chaining can make the process of formulating a plan more efficient than forward chaining.
- Backward chaining in this way starts with the goal state, which is the set of conditions the agent wishes to achieve in carrying out its plan. It now examines this state and sees what actions could lead to it.
- For example, if the goal state involves a block being on a table, then one possible action would be to place that block on the table.
- This action might not be possible from the start state, and so further actions need to be added before this action in order to reach it from the start state.
- In this way, a plan can be formulated starting from the goal and working back toward the start state.
- The benefit in this method is particularly clear in situations where the first state allows a very large number of possible actions.
- In this kind of situation, it can be very inefficient to attempt to formulate a plan using forward chaining because it involves examining every possible

action, without paying any attention to which action might be the best one to lead to the goal state.

- Backward chaining ensures that each action that is taken is one that will definitely lead to the goal, and in many cases this will make the planning process far more efficient.

- Comparing Forward and Backward Chaining

  - Let us use an example to compare forward and backward chaining. In this case, we will revert to our use of symbols for logical statements, in order to clarify the explanation, but we could equally well be using rules about elevators or the weather.

Rules:

Rule 1 A ^ B → C Rule 2 A → D Rule 3 C ^ D → E
Rule 4 B ^ E ^ F → G Rule 5 A ^ E → H Rule 6 D ^ E ^ H → I
Facts:
Fact 1 A
Fact 2 B
Fact 3 F
Goal:
Our goal is to prove H.

- First let us use forward chaining. As our conflict resolution strategy, we will fire rules in the order they appear in the database, starting from Rule 1.
- In the initial state, Rules 1 and 2 are both triggered. We will start by firing Rule 1, which means we add C to our fact database. Next, Rule 2 is fired, meaning we add D to our fact database.
- We now have the facts A, B, C, D, F, but we have not yet reached our goal, which is G.
- Now Rule 3 is triggered and fired, meaning that fact E is added to the database.
- As a result, Rules 4 and 5 are triggered. Rule 4 is fired first, resulting in Fact G being added to the database, and then Rule 5 is fired, and Fact H is added to the database.
- We have now proved our goal and do not need to go on any further.
- This deduction is presented in the following table:

- Now we will consider the same problem using backward chaining. To do so, we will use a goals database in addition to the rule and fact databases.
- In this case, the goals database starts with just the conclusion, H, which we want to prove. We will now see which rules would need to fire to lead to this conclusion.
- Rule 5 is the only one that has H as a conclusion, so to prove H, we must prove the antecedents of Rule 5, which are A and E.
- Fact A is already in the database, so we only need to prove the other antecedent, E. Therefore, E is added to the goal database. Once we have

proved E, we now know that this is sufficient to prove H, so we can remove H from the goals database.

- So now we attempt to prove Fact E. Rule 3 has E as its conclusion, so to prove E, we must prove the antecedents of Rule 3, which are C and D.
- Neither of these facts is in the fact database, so we need to prove both of them. They are both therefore added to the goals database. D is the conclusion of Rule 2 and Rule 2's antecedent, A, is already in the fact database, so we can conclude D and add it to the fact database.
- Similarly, C is the conclusion of Rule 1, and Rule 1's antecedents, A and B, are both in the fact database. So, we have now proved all the goals in the goal database and have therefore proved H and can

stop.

-

This process is represented in the table below:

- In this case, backward chaining needed to use one fewer rule. If the rule database had had a large number of other rules that had A, B, and F as their antecedents, then forward chaining might well have been even more inefficient.
- In general, backward chaining is appropriate in cases where there are few possible conclusions (or even just one) and many possible facts, not very many of which are necessarily relevant to the conclusion.
- Forward chaining is more appropriate when there are many possible conclusions.
- The way in which forward or backward chaining is usually chosen is to consider which way an expert would solve the problem. This is particularly appropriate because rule-based reasoning is often used in **expert systems**.

9 798889 862376

Printed by Libri Plureos GmbH in Hamburg,
Germany